MW00936749

Only in Iceland!

A Quirky Chronicle

Asifa Kanji

D. Drury & Sons, Publishers

London ✦ Berkeley ✦ Hilo ✦ Ashland

Copyright © 2017 by Asifa Kanji

All rights reserved.

This is my personal story. The views expressed in this book are the author's alone. Some of the names have been changed in the book.

Proceeds from the sale of this book will be donated to various charities of the author's choice

Inquiries and comments may be sent to:
ddruryandsonspub@gmail.com

ISBN-13: 978-1977943897

ISBN-10: 1977943896

To David, with deep love and gratitude.

There are no foreign lands.
It is the traveler only who is foreign.

-Robert Louis Stevenson

Contents

Circumnavigation of Iceland (map)   vi

Kissing Cousins   1

Why Iceland   2

Day One   3

Day Two - I want to go Home   7

Lisabet and the Isafjordur's Elves   17

The Imperfect Storm   25

The Hrisey Troll   28

Christmas, and the Geology of Stupid Trolls   34

Day Eight   39

Beautiful Iceland   40

Watch the Whales   44

Damn the Dam   47

The Beer Day   50

Silly, stupid tourists   52

I live and you will live   55

Search and Rescue Heroes   59

Homeward Bound   61

Reflections   62

Acknowledgments   65

Iceland

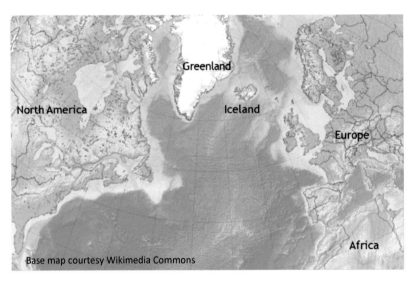

Base map courtesy Wikimedia Commons

Kissing Cousins

Did you know that Icelanders have an incest-prevention smart phone app? I had wondered about how a population of 335,000, nearly all of them with common descent from a group of 9th-century Viking settlers, kept their blue-eyed, blonde-haired teenagers from kissing their cousins. When I asked our guide about it, she said, "Oh there is a phone app for that." Well silly me for not thinking of the obvious. I googled "Icelandic date app." Sure enough, the Islediga-App's slogan: *Bump the app before you bump in bed,* popped up. It allows any Icelander to see just how closely related their date is simply by touching phones. It even has an *Incest Prevention Alarm* that notifies users if the person he or she is bumping with is too closely related!

Only in Iceland could one do this. They have an online database that holds the full genealogy of 720,000 Icelanders, living and deceased. It was assembled by combining old Icelandic genealogy books and church records for almost the entire population, stretching back more than 300 years. The Icelandic sagas, written about 1,000 years ago, all begin with page after page of genealogy.

What a frightfully formidable feat it must have been to create the *Islendingabok,* or Book of Icelanders, when each of the parents and their kids can and often do have totally different last names. A surname in Iceland is simply their father's first name, suffixed with either *son* for boys or *dóttir* for girls, based on a patronymic system that goes back to the time of the Vikings. My name in Iceland would have been *Asifa Johnsdottir* (John being the first name of my dad), and my brother would have been *Mahmud*

Johnson. My dad would be *John Janson* and my mum, Gulshan *Mohammedsdottir* (Mohammed was her dad's name). Four different surnames in the same family instead all of us being Kanjis!

Curiosity had me browsing the phonebook. What a surprise! People are listed in order of the person's first name, followed by surnames and addresses, and in some cases, profession. You'd better know where Bjork Gudlaughsdottir lives if you want to call her.

What a quirky country. I had no idea that this was just the beginning of the many zany stories I was to hear on this trip.

Why Iceland?

Why Iceland? Because traveling to Mount Everest would have been too much of a detour, not to mention that I'm too soft in body and mind to scale it. Iceland was on the way to London, where I had to go on business and visit family. I had only one preconceived idea of this amoeba-like island whose fingers stretch almost to that dotted line that is the Arctic Circle: Iceland promised raw beauty, a place where one cannot take anything for granted. I wanted to hike its craggy coast, feel the winds smack me, and play with the puffins in the icy north.

I surfed the net, looking for travel companies that offered loads of hiking in small groups, with minimum touring in coaches and minimum time in urban centers. Of course, I wanted someone else to schlep my luggage too. The Road Scholar *Dramatic Iceland by Foot and by Sea: A Circumnavigation* offered just that. There were only 12 in our group, all kindred spirits, though there were some 200 other passengers aboard the *Ocean Diamond*, an expedition boat with no casinos. For entertainment we attended lectures in the evenings on geology, bird life and the history and culture of Iceland. Was this too cushy an adventure? It didn't turn out to be.

Iceland was full of surprises - I had absolutely no clue what I was in for. I found magic, humor, beauty and friendship. I danced amongst the elves and the trolls. I weathered a storm, climbed volcanoes and soaked in the Blue Lagoon. Indeed, I was slapped by the wind and found myself to be an unwelcomed visitor as I traipsed through the nesting grounds of the Arctic Terns.

Day One

Luxuriating in the warm waters of the Blue Lagoon just an hour after we landed at Reykjavik was just what my flight-weary, limp body craved. Any remnant travel malaise dissolved into the turquoise mineral-rich water. I'm sure that it removes wrinkles

as well as curing foggy brain. At lunch, life got better still when a plateful of freshly steamed cod with cauliflower, barley and fennel, all splashed with a demi-glace sauce, was placed in front of me to savor. It didn't bother me one bit that the Blue Lagoon's restaurant could have been easily mistaken for a sanatorium dining room. It was crowded with barefoot patrons dressed in institutional white terry-towel robes. When the vanilla orange crème brulée was served, I knew it was going to be a fabulous trip.

Oops! I spoke too soon.

By the time we checked into our hotel in the afternoon, my husband David was feeling feverish, nauseous, had a tummy ache, and was constipated all at once. His home remedy -- sit outside in the cold and smoke a pipe. Even though he resembled a wet noodle, he insisted on joining our travel mates for dinner. He barely touched the welcome banquet. He was wilting in his chair. Plan B to cure what ailed him was simply to go to bed and sleep it off. I lived in hope.

Blue Lagoon Dining Room

Let's Soak!

Day Two - I want to go Home

A field trip through the Golden Circle our itinerary promised. Field trip indeed. It was more like running the Rekyavik environs tourist gauntlet by minibus. Forty minutes at Gullfoss, the Golden Waterfall; thirty minutes at Thingvellir National Park, home to Iceland's first parliament, established by the Vikings in 930 AD. Thirty minutes at Geysir, the scorching spouting spring after which all geysers have derived their name. Whew! And six hours of driving. No time to contemplate the wonder that is Iceland. The wonder that, almost eleven hundred years ago, a pack of quarrelsome chieftains, always quick to pick up their swords, looked for a better way to coexist by creating a National Assembly.

At Thingvellir, we stood briefly on the very site where they made laws and judged crimes. It was right here in the year 1000 where the respected pagan law speaker Thorgeir Thorkelsson gave a famous speech which basically said, "Look here folks, just follow the king's wishes and get baptized for the sake of avoiding war. But privately you can worship your pagan gods, eat horse flesh, and expose your children at birth if you choose." Yes, infanticide was practiced. And so it came to pass that Iceland became Christian.

Thingvellir was the site of their parliament for over 300 years. They created laws and argued and voted on legal cases. These heartless plunderers and philanderers of yore now believed in law and order! Well not quite. More often than not, they reverted to the Viking way of resolving issues, leaving the surrounding fields soaking in blood.

Thingvellir in the good old days

Theft carried a death penalty, but murder didn't. In fact, as retaliation for effrontery or insult, killing was absolutely honorable. Thieves were beheaded, and those found guilty of witchcraft were drowned to reduce the risk of their ghosts making trouble. Women who committed adultery were tied up in a sack and flung into the famous "drowning pool." We were told that back in the sixteenth century this pool was much deeper and more turbulent than it is today. What tormented ghosts must inhabit this place! Too cold to linger, I blew a prayer in the wind for the tortured souls.

It was a miserable grey icy day, but that was not all. We had to scramble through throngs of photo-snapping tourists all trying their utmost to capture that National Geographic-worthy shot of Nature in the raw -- the kind that leaves the viewer with the delusion that there was just the photographer and the butterflies to witness God's own amazing creation. It was a challenging pursuit. Busloads of tourists smashed in and out of viewing platforms like waves on a beach at high tide. Yes indeed, the world has discovered Iceland. This year alone has seen over two million visitors coming to an island slightly smaller than Cuba. It was a little crowded, I'd say.

If this was the prelude to our vacation, what was going to be in store for the rest of the days? Maybe this was a $7000 mistake, or maybe it would turn into one of life's adventures that we would only appreciate if we survive to tell the tale. Time would tell, but today I was powered by misery. The cold wind kept me moving at a furious clip, if only to prevent my blood from forming icicles in my veins.

"Hotels are springing up like weeds after a rain," said Groa, our guide. She was concerned about the future and integrity of her country. It was less than ten years ago that the economy tanked when the global real estate bubble burst. "Until then," she told us," Icelanders had been living it up, buying bigger houses, faster cars, the latest gizmos, all on credit." Jobs and money poured in, fuelled by the establishment of a NATO base there, manned first by British and then by American soldiers.

In 2007, the Americans pulled their troops out. A year later, the bubble burst and the government said, "No bailout." All the country's main banks collapsed, and living standards spiraled down fast. Icelanders were angry, disappointed and broke. Eventually foreign banks took the hit to keep Iceland's finances afloat.

How did they rebuild their economy? Through tourism.

Gulfoss

They marketed their beautiful country to the world, seducing travelers from here, there and everywhere to experience the wonder that is Iceland. The campaign has been immensely successful, and here I was, a crumb in that crush of tourists.

It was not all misery on that first day out. Lunch was an incredible experience. The restaurant was actually inside a mega-greenhouse where row after row of tomato plants kissed the ceiling before draping down almost to the floor, heavily pregnant with ripe red tomatoes ready for picking. Geothermally heated water was piped in, and hydroelectric power fed the array of sun lamps. The lunch menu was simple, homemade tomato soup and umpteen varieties of fresh baked bread. The drinks menu read like a Catholic litany: Bloody Mary, Virgin Mary, Healthy Mary, Happy Mary and Green Mary. Schnapps was served in a hollowed-out tomato. And for desert, tomato ice cream and tomato apple pie. Never mind the steely cold skies outside, in here it was sunny and cozy. Bees hummed and went about their business - they had too many tomatoes to pollinate to bother with us mortals. It was a finger lickin' experience until we had to leave this tropical womb of artificial sunshine and warmth to venture back into the freezing Icelandic summer. We still had more places to see.

What was I thinking when I booked this tour? Twenty-four hours of daylight does not translate into bikini weather. The average summer temperature is 50 degrees, but they forgot to include wind chill. "Dress in layers," our travel agent said. I had all of them on, but oh the wind and rain showed no mercy to my aging bones. As Groa related to us the history of the first parliament, all I heard was my chattering teeth. I wanted desperately to run back and seek shelter in the bus. It did not comfort me to know that the Icelanders have 56 different words for wind.

David crashed just as soon as we reached the hotel. I went in search of food. Dinner tonight was not included. I looked at the room service menu and quickly ascertained that this was a good night to fast. An ice cream bar was $20; hamburgers ran for $28, and a cheese plate cost $22. Beer was $11. Water from the tap was directly from melting glaciers, and that was free. Delicious!

I discovered that at the bar they had a self service table with cups of bubbling hot pea soup for $12.50. I splurged and bought two cups. David described it as like eating library paste. I wonder how he knows what that tastes like? In fairness to the soup chef, David could not taste much. He went to bed at 6:30pm and slept for 14 hours. I decided to go out and walk the streets of Reykjavik, the smallest and northernmost European capital.

Reykjavik Cathedral

Small, colorful happy houses lining their streets.

Quaint boutiques galore begging to be browsed.

Bustling bars, cozy restaurants, all so precious.

I was strolling the down skimpy streets of a miniature Scandinavian town.

Window shopping was a delight,

The price tags, very scary.

Blue Jeans for $165. Gas was about $7.50 a gallon.

Early bird two course dinners at a modest looking restaurant ran around $60 per person.

Oh my, maybe the hotel prices weren't so bad after all.

I loved the lake where lovers sat, and little blonde girls and boys chased birds. I stopped there to breathe the exquisitely clean Icelandic air. The skies had cleared, the wind had dropped, life had improved considerably. If only my husband would recover, I couldn't wish for more happiness than that.

* * * *

Whatever bug afflicted David, it soon became greatly discouraged - no doubt it was smoked to death. He was almost back to his old self when we boarded the Ocean Diamond, an expedition boat to circumnavigate Iceland. For the next nine days, with the boat as our hotel, we would forsake the tourist trails for sheep and goat trails. This was what we came here for, to hike in many different parts of the country.

The Ocean Diamond

As we sailed out of the harbor, Groa pointed to the docked coastguard ship. "That's one-third of our military right there," she said. The coastguard has three ships to guard their fishing rights. No wonder they can afford to spend 60% of the country's budget on education alone, and offer free health care to everyone. As

long as she was boasting, she said that Iceland actually had a near-zero crime rate. The police were unarmed, and the president rode his bike around town. When their former president's wife was found to be involved in the Panama Papers scandal, he had the decency to resign, our guide Groa told us. Was this a back-handed commentary on our President? Mercifully, the conversations never disintegrated to discussing American politics. That alone felt like a vacation in itself. Freezing my butt off was a welcome break from political discourse.

Lisabet and the Isafjordur Elves

When crazy, funny, headstrong Lisabet boarded our van, one of the first things she said was "You are all adults, but in case you don't know, you should take your jackets off and strip down. Otherwise, when we leave the bus, you will freeze." She hesitated for a moment then giggled in embarrassment. "I'm sorry, I can't help it, I am a mother of four."

Lisabet was our local guide for the day. Having introduced herself, she told us "I love gossip and storytelling, so if you want facts, you'll have to ask a historian." My kind of guide – *Never let the truth get in the way of a good story, for all my stories are true. And some of them actually happened.* I'm already looking forward to the day, as I have had enough of the population-of-Iceland-is-335,000....." kind of guides.

She was dressed in a dark-chocolate brown crocheted short skirt with rainbow stripes woven along the hem, chartreuse tights, blue sneakers and a scarf of many colors that she wrapped around her head and neck. I couldn't help but be drawn to her because she was precisely herself, no more, no less.

"I am one of three Lisabets in Iceland. My grandmother was the first" she said, "which is the only reason the naming board approved my parents' petition to name me after her."

"Really? You have to get permission to name your child?"

"Yes, if the name you choose is not on the list of approved Icelandic names," she told us. "Most of them are really ugly and old fashioned. Who would name their baby *Lofthaena*?"

Dunno, but I know a rock star who named his daughter *Moon Unit*. Indeed there is an official list of approved names, and Moon Unit is not on it, but then again neither is Asifa. Such a name couldn't be declined in accordance with Icelandic grammar. "Rejected," the panel would declare, and the child would not have a birth certificate until the parents conformed.

* * * *

From Isafjordur, where we were docked, it was a 40 minute van ride to Onundarfjorder. The road went through the fabled Botns & Breidadals tunnel, the one the elves held hostage. Yes you read right -- it's another of those only-in-Iceland stories that Lisabet told us about.

"There is an Elf Committee in the town." Lisabet didn't need the van's microphone to be heard. "These people have spent five years at university learning to communicate with the elves." No kidding, there is an Elf University? She must be pulling our legs. Immediately I googled it. This last year of American politics has made fact checking a habit. Indeed there is an Elf school in Reykjavik, not for elves, but for people who want to get closer to elves. How I wish we could have visited it. And yes, there are people who really believe in elves, or at least they won't actively deny their existence. Unlike the mischievous Irish elves with green curled up pointy tip boots and green top hats, Icelandic elves are serious little people.

---

[1] http://europa.eu/youth/is/article/117/18510_en

18

According to Fanney Magna Karlsdóttir[1]:

Iceland's version of elves are called 'Huldufólk,' which translates as 'Hidden People'. They are invisible beings who live inside rocks and communicate occasionally with humans through their dreams. In appearance they look like humans, except they dress mostly in old fashioned Icelandic clothing. They farm and fish like humans do, and probably go about their daily lives in much the same way as humans. They are generally not considered hostile but have been known to occasionally steal human children, swapping them for old, disgruntled elvish men. However, those who do good by the Hidden People are awarded generously.

The origins of the Hidden People are very unclear since there are so many different stories out there, most of them deeply rooted in Christianity. However, there is one story that seems to stand out as the most popular, and it relates to Adam and Eve's children.

The Hidden People were believed to be the children of Adam and Eve. In anticipation of God's visit, Eve decided to clean up her children. She didn't have enough time to clean all of them, so she made the dirty children hide to ensure that God would only see the ones who were clean. God of course knew what she had done and was quite infuriated. God then declared: "What man hides from God, God will hide from man."[2]These children came to be the Hidden People's ancestors.

Lisabet went on to say that the Elf committee in Isafjordur

---

[2]*Ashliman, D. L. "Origin of the Hidden People: Two Legends from Iceland by Jón Arnason". D. L. Ashliman's folktexts. Retrieved 2008-09-18.*

recommended a delay in starting the tunnel until they obtained the permission and blessings of the resident elves. Months passed. Finally the Mayor became antsy enough to say the hell with this, and ordered the work to begin with or without elfin approval.

Wellll . . . . In the first week, most of the machinery broke down, accidents happened, and all the townsfolk blamed the Mayor for the disastrous start, forcing him to call a halt to the work. The committee, after communing with the elves, recommended that the Mayor go on national TV and publicly say I am sorry to them, which he duly did. A couple of days after the apology, the committee announced "Good to go now. The elves have accepted the apology." The rest of the tunnel construction proceeded without incident.

I imagined the elves going back to their kids and telling them how they made silly humans apologize on public television, and having a good laugh over it.

Truth or Fiction? I tried googling the story - the Internet has everything, doesn't it? I found exactly the same story written by another travel blogger who also had Lisabet as his or her guide. I also found other stories of work coming to a halt because of elves, and yes there are people who really do talk to and negotiate with the elves on behalf of the human race. Who knew? I thought kind thoughts about them, just as I did for Madame Pele in Hawaii.

On that day we were supposed to do an eight mile hike through the jagged mountains and be awed by spectacular views of Isafjordur and Onundarfjordur.

Onundarfjordur

Diaphanous mist turned into soupy fog and back to mist. The two danced so eloquently with the dizzyingly steep mountains, with a splash of sunshine working its own magic as the light shone and dimmed. It had rained all night, and the wind wanted to dance too, but to its own frenetic rhythm. Witnessing Earth's own drama had me planted in this sparsely inhabited area in the West Fjords, where itty bitty villages are strung together by dirt roads. I didn't notice the thousands of arctic terns, performing haphazard aerial stunts behind me, until I heard Lisabet shout. "Hold your hiking poles up above your heads or you'll have your brains cut open by the dive bombers," she sniggered. Her idea of an authentic Icelandic experience was to have us run past the nesting grounds. Sure enough, a couple of squawking, scolding terns attacked the tip of my pole. *Kria! Kria! Kria!* they screeched. I kept an eye on David, who chose to ignore local wisdom and defy Nature by scampering unprotected through the charging battalion of Krias, the bird's name in Icelandic.

"You have a choice of braving the storm in the mountains, playing swamp soccer, or walking on the road through this valley to one of the rare white sand beaches in Iceland," said Lisabet. Swamp Soccer? The very idea of jumping into the smuddy swamps and kicking a soccer ball sounded deranged. "It's really fun," Lisabet insisted. "We dress in all kinds of bizarre costumes when we play." The group politely declined. Privately, I entertained thoughts of Icelanders gone crackers - must be those long winters. We chose the road to the beach.

Swamp soccer, anyone?

Lisabet was full of stories of how their lives here were punctuated by blizzards and avalanches and flash floods, forcing them to evacuate. They all have an emergency bag ready to go. Each household has a go-to friend or family member, should catastrophe strike. For her family, they go to her grandmother's. Schools and roads are closed for as much as a week at a time, and work stops until they get the all-clear to return home. By the same token, she has extra duvets and mattresses and emergency rations should disaster strike on the other side of the fjord. Evidently Iceland has some pretty good warning systems, making evacuations possible. They have also built a 66 foot high avalanche dam to protect the settlements here, and now there is a tunnel that has also eased winter travel.

I kept pace with Lisabet as we hiked through the valley, not wanting to miss a word of what she had to say. The storm unfurled all around us on the surrounding mountains. Time to don my rain pants, coats and gaiters. She waited for the group to catch up. I asked her if children could take on their mother's name. "Oh yes, the naming police do allow that" she said, and launched into a story.

Just before her second child was born she insisted, in the midst of her contractions, that she was *not* going to squeeze this kid out until her husband would agree that it be named after her -- Lisabetsdottir. "I'm doing all the work, and she should have my name!" she told her frazzled husband. "At that moment, when I was screaming in agony, my husband agreed to everything I said. With the third child, we decided to give her both our names. So she is Gudrun LisabetGunnarsdottir, and for the fourth child's last name they used, GunnarLisabetsson."

All was well until they went on a driving tour of Eastern Europe.

They wanted to cross the border into a small Russian town that was reputed to have the world's best ice cream. "The Russian border immigration guys treated us as though we were trafficking children. They wouldn't believe that we were one family, as we all had different last names. Then one guard looked at my eldest son and asked him, Are those your parents?" The boy, who must have inherited some of his mother's personality, was quick to say 'Nyhet. Never seen them before in my life.' "None of us ate ice cream that day."

Onundarfjordur

I wonder what happens now, as Iceland accepts refugees and immigrants. How will the strictly enforced naming conventions hold? It is a major transition time for this insular community, as they are challenged to become more multicultural. My own thoughts are that it's good for the gene pool, and it won't be long before they won't need Islediga-App's Incest Prevention Alarm anymore.

There was no Good Humor man selling ice cream at the beach. Hot chocolate would have gone down very well, except there was no one selling that either. In the land of fjords, ice and fire, I could see why this small white sand beach is a treasured gift. "We come here to look at the horizon," Lisabet said. When you live in valleys with sheer rocky walls rising to the sky, seeing the horizon is very special. Intellectually I understood, but emotionally I couldn't fathom why anybody would want to live here at all. The day visit was quite enough to fill my soul with the beauty that is Isafjordur, but live here? Never.

Back at the ship, I had the most welcome hot shower ever to warm up my innards. I was quite ready for that glass of wine. Tonight, we would put on our party togs. We were to sup in the private dining room with the Captain -- or maybe not.

The Imperfect Storm

Our ship was steaming towards the Arctic Circle. Our destination? Grimsey Island, the puffin haven. They had barely served the drinks in the fancy dining room, when "Holy Shi-ugar! " and other expletives fell out of our collective mouths. We had almost been knocked out of our chairs. A 25 foot wave had smashed against our boat. "Creak!" The boat cried as it tried to right itself, but not fast enough to avoid another slap, and then another. Glasses went flying, beer and wine spoiled the crisp white table cloths. The staff barely kept their footing, moving like tipsy ballet dancers, balancing trays of food above their heads. I guessed the Captain was a little too busy to stop by and dine with us.

Passenger after passenger abandoned his or her dinner, and clumsily dos-y-do'ed out of the dining room. With just a handful of us left, swaying with the boat, I was trying with all the dignity I could muster to direct forkfuls of salmon into my mouth. Timing was everything, or else greasy fish flakes would end up in my nostrils.

Trying to sound nonchalant, I asked the head steward, "On a scale of zero to 10, how bad is this storm?"

"Not bad," he said. "One time we were down in Antarctica and a wave actually crashed the window open. The dining room, the galley, everything flooded."

I nervously glanced at the briny water raining down the panes of the window next to me. *I should move my seat,* I thought. *But if I dared to stand up now, I might splatter across the floor like the beer and wine.* Another wave, another undulation rocked and rolled us. *No, I'll stay where I am, the only way to hang on to what is left of my poise.*

"So what happened"? I asked the steward.

"My first priority was to deliver food to the cabins. Nobody had eaten. We took bread, cheese, bottled water and fruit from the galley to where it was dry enough to make sandwiches. The next day when we came into port, we had to abort the cruise."

With that thought, David and I decided we'd eaten as much as we could stomach and tried to make our way to the cabin. We stumbled down the ship's corridors as though we were totally soused, zig zagging from one wall to another, hanging on to the hand rails, trying to hold ourselves upright as much as we could.

For a few moments we stopped to watch the waves from the more sheltered stern deck. Instantaneously my adrenalin started pumping frenetically. Every cell in my body was on full alert. This was no Hollywood special effect. This was real. We could drown. *Run Asifa, run!* Yet my feet wouldn't move. The wave was growing. It was coming right at me – well, actually at the side of the boat. It didn't matter. I think I wet my pants. Just in time, our boat climbed that crest. I ran inside where neither wind nor water could catch me. At least not yet.

I loved the thrill of the storm, feared it, was frozen by it and eventually surrendered to it, by going to bed and feeling its rhythm and power as it lifted the boat onto the wave's crest and let it slide down into the abyss before the next one hit. We had to trust that the *Ocean Diamond* would hold together and the captain knew what he was doing. Just in case, I had my life jacket within arm's reach.

I admit to entertaining romantic notions of floating in the Arctic sea in a dinghy, waiting to be rescued. Of course I would be rescued. How else would I get to tell my story and have a movie made from it?

Suddenly all was calm.

"I am afraid because of the storm we will not be crossing the Arctic Circle," the captain announced, and in the way of an apology, he went on about safety coming first. He found a sheltered place in one of the fjords, where we anchored for the night. "Hope you have a restful night," he said.

For me this was a true arctic experience. Thank you Thor, the Norse storm god of thunder, lightning, oak trees, protection of humanity, strength, hallowing, healing, and fertility! A multi-tasking God.

The Hrisey Troll

What do you do with a boatload of passengers whose stomachs are still roiling? You put them in a Zodiac and deposit them on terra firma, ASAP. Taking a brisk walk in the chilly air was a sure cure for wobbly legs and nervous digestive tracts.

When we landed on Hrisey Island the next morning, I so badly wanted to follow one of the other passengers, who was leaning on her walker as she rolled herself slowly towards the island's only cafe. She had been courageous enough to climb down into the Zodiac with her weak and compromised legs, and had landed in a puddle of icy arctic water. Cold and wet equals total misery in my book. I shivered for her. I wanted to join her and while away the hours, sipping hot chocolate, and stuffing my gob with home baked pastries. *After the hike we'll stop there*, I promised my pleasure-princess self.

Hrisey (population 120) had the dubious distinction of being

Iceland's quarantine center for imported pigs and cattle. Over forty years ago, when they opened the center, Icelandic horses and sheep -- which are never interbred with foreigners -- were taken off the island to keep them safe from species-hopping diseases. This left more vegetation for ground-nesting bird species. Terns, ptarmigans and eiders are among the many feathered friends that love to hang out here. It was a stunning walk across the flat moorlands and on to the trail that ran alongside the water's edge. Rocky, sculpted cliffs spilled into the water. I saw gulls nested in crevices of the sheer walls. Magical Ley Lines, the earth's invisible energy lines, crisscross this very island. "Just stop and feel the energy," one local said to me. I did.

At that very moment a rainbow appeared to light the rocky wall on the other side of the straits. Ley Lines or not, I was delighted and filled with joy deep enough to feel blessed to be alive and a part of this magical Universe. I was ready to experience the extraordinary. With that frame of mind, I hiked on, with eider-ducks and terns for company.

Sign on the Hrisey trail

I stopped dead on the trail. I swear I saw a troll, the frozen-in-rock kind. *How sad he looked. Maybe his heart had been broken.* I could imagine this ugly but gentle giant leading a lonely life in his pitch-black cave, looking forward to those moments in summer when he could peek secretly at the beautiful young woman who would bathe au natural in the waters by his dark dwelling. He would inhale her beauty and dream of domestic bliss with the lovely one. He could only yearn, for he knew if he stepped out into the sunlight, he would instantly turn to stone. Sunlight is the trolls' Achilles' heel.

I had heard one story where a male troll tried to charm a human girl. Alas, the girl was revolted by him. Nevertheless, he persisted with amorous ardor. In the end she told him to bugger off and go turn into a stone, which he immediately did. Just like that, abracadabra. How I would love that power. I can think of at least one guy who could benefit from turning into stone, and it is not my husband.

In my childhood, the only troll I knew was the terrifying terrible troll called Trevor, who lived under a bridge and wanted to eat the Billy Goats Gruff. My dad would play the troll and I the Billy Goats. The game would always end up with my dad catching me and tickling me to pieces when I crossed our imaginary rickety rackety bridge. I loved it when he played the terrifying terrible troll called Trevor.

However, in my story of the frozen-in-the-rock-troll that I had just seen, I imagined that he got totally carried away by his fantasies and stepped out to propose to the beautiful human girl. Before a single word spluttered from his tongue, the sunlight splashed his face, turning him into stone. To this day, there he kneels, just a step away from his cave, for all eternity, waiting to propose to the beautiful one. Sorry, there is no moral to this story, except to tell stupid male trolls, *Know your boundaries.*

Will you marry me?

It was time to return. At the dock, waiting for the Zodiac to fetch us, our guide Groa was in tears -- good tears, the kind that flow when you are moved by kindness. "Remember the lady with the walker who got wet?" she asked.

"At the cafe, the owner lent her clothing and washed and dried her wet pants, and fed her home-baked cakes with a cup of steaming hot chocolate. So beautiful," she said as she wiped her eyes dry.

Hot chocolate! I had forgotten all about that. "I'd love a hot drink," I said out loud.

"*Brennivin* will warm you up more," said one of the townsmen who was hanging around the dock.

"Is it as good as the Norwegian Akevit?"

"Of course it is as good. It is better," the townsman replied. "Though I never tasted Akevit."

There was a rapid interchange in Icelandic between the ship's staff and him, and before we knew it, the townsman jumped in his ancient Subaru and drove off in great haste. Oh my goodness, did we offend him? Did I overstep some cultural boundary?

"The people of this village are very special," Groa said again. I assumed that she was still thinking of the cafe owner's hospitality.

Still I wondered, what if the woman with the walker had been an immigrant, a person of color, would she have been given the same treatment in this small town? Immigrant issues are getting a lot of airtime and people are split, Groa had told me. Iceland is taking some of the Syrian refugees and immigration has increased dramatically, especially from Poland. "There are not enough people in our country to make beds and clean rooms for the tourists. Icelanders don't want to do those jobs. I don't know why people are so afraid, or what they are afraid of." She herself was thrilled to bits that her son's bestie was Iranian, and that her boy was growing up without prejudice and learning so much about world cultures.

Just as the Zodiac was approaching the dock to pick us up, the Subaru pulled up and the townsman popped out, holding a half-empty bottle of *Brennivin.* He handed it to me to take a swig.

I did. A satisfying warm burn tickled my throat all the way down my chest. It felt so good, I had to take another. "Caraway. I taste caraway. "

"But is it better than the Norwegian stuff, yah?" The townsman waited for the judgment.

"It's so good that I think I'll buy a bottle and take it back to America with me," I said. And I did, even though I had to cash in my pension fund to do so.

The townsman grinned from ear to ear and helped me climb down into the Zodiac. He was willing to share his precious bottle with me - an immigrant, a person of color. Why would I ever doubt that the cafe proprietress wouldn't have done the same for me? That's just how people in this town are.

*   *   *   *

Brennivin, literally "burning wine," is made from fermented potato mash and is flavored with caraway seeds. It is the traditional drink for Iceland's 'ugly food festival[3],' Þorrablót -- a pagan tradition that was revived in the sixties. It begins on the 23rd of January, which is Bóndadagur (Husband's Day), and ends a month later on Konudagur (Women's Day), marking that special time of year known as *Þorrablót,* when Icelanders feast on ugly food like boiled sheep's head, pickled ram's testicles, blood pudding, liver pudding, and putrefied shark. Only in Iceland! Fortunately for us, we missed this culinary assault. I too, would be guzzling spirits if for no other reason but to disinfect my insides after eating testicles and rotten fish.

---

[3] http://icelandictimes.com/icelands-ugly-food-festival-thorrablot-is-here/

View from Mt. Hverfell

Christmas & the Geology of Stupid Trolls

"Trolls are big, stupid and greedy," our local guide said as we climbed up the steep slope of Mount Hverfell, a desolate volcanic crater that commands sweeping views of the area from its rim. W*hat! My dad wasn't stupid and greedy, he was a fun troll and I loved him.* I kept my thoughts to myself.

Icelandic trolls live deep in the uninhabitable highlands, coming out to make mischief only when it is dark outside. They like the taste of flesh, and are known to lure unsuspecting humans into their caves with spells, magic potions, or simply by taking them captive. They steal and eat misbehaving children, parents tell their naughty kids. Fortunately, trolls have a reputation of being stupid, so quick-thinking humans can easily free themselves of troll enchantments. Phew!

We continued our walk to Dimmuborgir or "black castles." This is a vast, 2000 year old field of contorted volcanic pillars, some six or seven stories high.

"The Christmas trolls live here," our guide said. I perked up immediately. "You have to wait to December to see them," he laughed. He cued me to look for the dead trolls. Once he had pointed out a rocky troll face in the lava outcroppings, everywhere I looked I saw troll faces and limbs - a veritable graveyard of unburied trolls.

Dimmuborgir formations

The magnificent rock formations we were looking at were, of course, massive armies of petrified trolls who had suffered the harsh fate of the sun. Given the sheer number of lava formations, the island must have been jammed with careless trolls. My favorite story was about an exasperated troll. The bells of a monastery were driving him insane, and at nightfall, he set out to tear them down. As it was a massive undertaking, he totally lost track of time. The sun came up, and booboom! He is now the Hvítserkur cliff of the Vatnesnes peninsula in northwest Iceland.

"Do you believe in trolls?" I asked our guide. "Yes," he said. "And I believe in Santa Claus too."

Every child believes in trolls, especially at Christmas time. In Iceland they have not one but thirteen gift-bearing Yule Lads. There's *Sheep Cote Clod, Gully Hawk, Stubby* and *Spoon Licker*. There's also *Pot Scraper, Bowl Licker, Door Slammer and Skyr Gobbler*. They are followed by *Sausage Swiper, Window Peeper, Doorway Sniffer,* and *Meat hook*. But the most loved of all is *Candle Beggar*. He leaves behind the biggest gifts on Christmas Eve.

I have a hard time remembering the names of the seven dwarfs and Santa's reindeers, and to think Icelandic kids have to remember them by their local names:

Stekkjastaur, Giljagaur, Stúfur, Þvörusleikir, Pottaskefill, Askasleikir, Hurðaskellir, Skyrgámur, Bjúgnakrækir, Gluggagægir, Gáttaþefur, Ketkrókur, Kertasníkir.

Our guide recited them off like the multiplication tables.

But the Christmas trolls of yore were ogres. They caused absolute mayhem at the farmsteads -- they were hideous, shockingly ill-bred shifty pilferers, stealing sausages, skyr (an Icelandic yoghurt) and pans. Warty face Spoon Licker licked spoons when the cook wasn't looking, while Door Banger spooked everyone by randomly slamming doors at night. They hid under the naughty kids' beds and tormented them. Every time a door banged or a light shone in the window, children would tremble with fear, trying hard to recall just how bad they had been. Would they be carried off and be cooked in a stew, like mamma and papa had told them over and over?

The thirteen Yule Lads, as they were collectively known, are the sons of Gryla. Gryla is a giant troll with hooves for feet and thirteen tails. She's always in a bad mood, due to her insatiable hunger for children, bad children. Each Christmas, Gryla comes down from her mountain dwelling to hunt for them, placing them in a sack and dragging them back to her cave, where she boils them alive for her favorite stew.

Kids became so unnerved at Christmas time that in 1746, a royal decree was issued banning parents from scaring their kids with Yule Lad stories. That was the beginning of the end for the traditional scary Christmas trolls in Iceland.

Today, the Yule lads have been repackaged in Santa outfits. While they are still pranksters, children love them and leave a shoe on the window sill every night for the twelve nights of Christmas. Good children receive a small gift from the Yule Lads, but bad children will find rotten potatoes in their shoes.

Misbehaving kids in Iceland aren't completely off the hook, however, because the old story of Grylla still survives. So maybe it's still not quite safe to come out from under the covers around Christmastime in Iceland . . at least if you have been naughty.

Troll stories aside, the geological story is equally mind-boggling.

Not only does Iceland squat atop a hot spot that spews up lava, it also straddles the Mid-Atlantic ridge, where the European and the North American tectonic plates are tearing the island apart at the speed of growing finger-nails, about an inch a year. At 20 million years old, it is one of the most volcanically active spots on earth. Because hot lava bubbles up under an enormous ice cap, hot springs and geothermal pools abound, as do flash floods, when all that pent up melted ice bursts out. Between earthquakes and 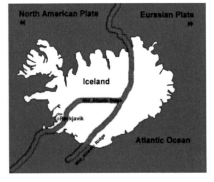 eruptions, ocean storms, gusty winds and terrifying avalanches, Iceland is as riotous as a pack of hyperactive kids let loose in a crystal shop.

Icelanders are quick to cash in on their geological inheritance, and not just for tourism. Geothermal heat and abundant hydroelectric power keep them toasty. In every town, naturally heated public pools complete with water slides and hot tubs keep the locals mellow and laughing. I didn't hesitate to change into my tankini and soak in the public baths, a great place to meet and chat with locals.

The bad news was the local gentry didn't miss an opportunity to ask why, in a country whose population exceeds 350 million, Trump was the best we could come up with. I fumbled. If anybody has a good, succinct and witty answer, I would love to hear it.

Day Eight

We were running out of clean clothes. Weren't we lucky that on that very day the ship's staff left a flier on our beds attached to two small cloth bags. "A special on laundry!" the notice said: $39 for one load, $75 for two, and $99 for three. Yikes! If this was a special offer, how much do they charge normally?

There has to be a Laundromat at one of the ports. I was on a mission. We found it at a youth hostel in Akureyri. At $9 per wash load and the same to dry it for 20 minutes, it seemed a bargain. With the money we saved, I signed up for a massage and life got even better.

Akureyri Youth Hostel & Eighteen Dollar Laundromat

Beautiful Iceland

More fabulous days of hiking -- let the pictures tell the story.

Berserkjahraum

Berserkjahraum

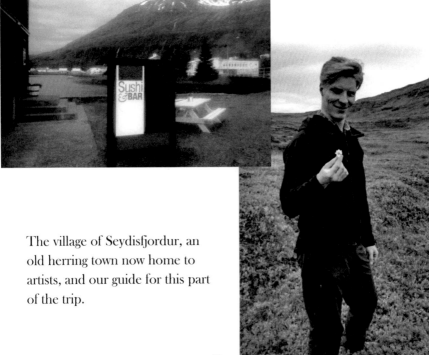

The village of Seydisfjordur, an
old herring town now home to
artists, and our guide for this part
of the trip.

Telephone booth sculpture commemorating laying of the cable
between Scotland and Iceland.   Below: Godafoss waterfall

Watch the Whales

Today, being on vacation was tediously hard work. It was one of those dreaded tour days.

Eat.

Hurry up and wait for your group to be called.

Tour Bus.

Whale Watch.

Eat.

Hurry up and wait for your group to be called.

Tour Bus.

Visit traditional farm.

Eat.

Attend lecture.

Fall asleep writing my journal.

Dear Tour Operator, please give me a ten-mile hike or a mountain to climb.

The promise of a story teller on board the bus kept me from abandoning the group field trip and taking a nap.

Husavik Harbor

A Good Catch!

We were in Husavik, the whale watching capital of Iceland. Here hotshot small boat captains chased after any visible flicker of a tail or water spout in the ocean for their photo-hungry gaggles of tourists. I was tormented. Though the tourist me mentally begged the whales to perform party tricks, my heart wanted to leave these amazing beings alone to live their lives.

With the excitement of a sportscaster reporting a goal, the spotter announced, "There's a whale!" The captain did a sharp turn and stepped on the gas, hurtling us towards the fountain that had collapsed back into the ocean, leaving not a trace behind. On the main deck, we rushed around, readying our cameras and binoculars, bunching up in the spot on the boat that offered the best view.

"There it is again!" someone yelled. Our gaggle was quick to reposition.

I was caught up in the excitement. Even jaded me held my breath as a big blue whale (is there any other kind?) glided in and out, in and out, flicking its flukes at us before gliding away. We saw him again and again, but only because we assiduously followed him -- or was it a her? To be in the presence of a such a humongous creature, bigger than a semi, yet moving so elegantly stirred wonder in my heart. I just watched, enjoyed being out at sea, feeling the wind whistle through my hoodie, and contemplating the watery world under our boat. No camera could capture the moment's ecstasy, which like a dewdrop in sunshine, evaporated just as soon as it could. The spotter would earn a good tip today.

Wooden ships at Husavik

Damn the Dam

"I was born here" said our guide, a middle-aged history teacher who had jumped on the tourism gravy train for a little extra income. "The Grenjadastadur people are leaders. We have been the first to do everything," he said. "We started the first Icelandic bank in 1850. 158 years later, in the crash of 2008, it was the only bank that did not go bankrupt. We are very proud of that."

We were on our way to the turf farm of Grenjadarstadur, which had been abandoned in 1932. Since then it has been restored and turned into a folk museum where actor/guides dressed in nineteenth century costume offered a glimpse into Iceland's traditional farming methods and living conditions. Those were the days when clothes had to be boiled; tiny beds were often shared by several people; the cows had to be milked and the butter churned in the freezing, unending dark months of winter. Someone joked that if Icelanders were lucky, summer would fall over a weekend. We had heard the same joke in Norway, years earlier. It drove home how tough one had to be to live here as subsistence farmers.

Museum farm at Grenjadarstadur

It was in this area that the first Icelandic co-op was born back in the latter part of the 19th century, because the farmers wanted freedom from various national monopolies that kept prices high. After 150 years the co-op finally shut its doors a few years after the market crashed.

Mister History Teacher/guide told us the famous story of the night they blew up the dam, right here on this river in northern Iceland that we were driving by.

"August 25, 1970, was a normal quiet night by river Laxá. But somewhere behind the darkness, beneath the silence, something extraordinary was about to happen. It was around midnight. A thunderous explosion jolted everybody."

The next morning, 125 farmers showed up at the police station to claim responsibility for the explosion, which had destroyed the small dam in the river. The farmers made it impossible for the authorities to single out the saboteurs. Why did they blow up the dam? It was a rebellion. The government wanted to build a much bigger one. All this natural area, and the farmlands we saw, would have been under water. It would have been an ecological disaster. The farmers wanted none of it, and the authorities, like authorities everywhere, were quite deaf; but they heard the explosion all right.

"It took 40 years before we actually found out the names of the three men who did it, of which two had already died," he said.

What made the Laxá conflict special was that those who resisted, succeeded. The planned dam was never built, and the area was saved and later protected by law. "This was the most remarkable and powerful event in the history of environmentalism in Iceland," as Sigurður Gizurarson, the bomber's defense lawyer, put it. Many people count it as the starting point of the environmental movement here.

Had they not blown up the dam, I suppose we might have had a boating excursion in the lake and would have never experienced this fragile but incredibly beautiful landscape.

Speaking of co-ops and monopolies, Costco has recently opened its first outlet in Reykjavik. Like many Icelanders, I wondered if this was the beginning of multinationals displacing local businesses, by luring customers with cheap Chinese doodads. Will dissidents dynamite the warehouse in protest, like they did the dam, or have modern day Icelanders succumbed to a softer and a more urban lifestyle, preferring to buy milk from a carton instead of milking the cow?

People from the Laxá area seem to take great pride in making a lifestyle out of hardship and deprivation. I couldn't help wondering whether it was people like them who voted to ban beer for all those years.

The Beer Day

It blew my mind that from January 1 1915 until March 1 1989 beer was banned in Iceland. Not hard spirits, not wine... Just beer.

Why oh why a beer ban? Here is what Icelandic blogger UselessGit had to say:[4]

Our benevolent government decided that selling beer would increase the risk of workers and children (someone was, indeed, thinking of them) being tempted by Bacchus. Strong liquor was bad, but people were trusted to avoid it if they were free of the devastating gateway booze that was beer. People were actually worried that if anyone tasted beer, they would immediately become addicted to alcohol.

One of our guides said he remembered being able to buy large containers of wort (unfermented beer) plastered with big caution labels: "Danger - Do NOT add sugar and yeast." Guess what he did when he took them home? He laughed at the memory. He also remembered the *beer bars* where they would spike the wort with Brennivin or vodka. "It was horrible." He scrunched his face as though he still could taste it.

---

[4] *(http://boards.straightdope.com/sdmb/showthread.php?t=362698)*

Prohibition and the beer ban have a quirky history in Iceland. In the beginning of the 1900s temperance movements were very popular all around the western world, and Iceland was no exception. Thus, it was no surprise that in a national election in 1908, over 60% of Icelanders voted for a complete ban on alcohol – although the ban didn't come into effect until 1915.

In 1922 wine was made legal again – but ONLY wines from Portugal and Spain. Exporting fish to Spain was big business, so when the Spaniards stopped buying Icelandic fish in retaliation for the ban on alcohol in 1915, Icelanders decided that maybe Iberian wine was okay to drink after all.

In 1935, the ban on strong liquor and spirits was lifted. But beer remained illegal. Beer was what the Danes drank, and since Iceland was engaged in a struggle for independence from Denmark (which they finally achieved in 1944), drinking beer was considered unpatriotic.

The British invaded Iceland in 1940 to protect it from the Nazis, and for obvious reasons, they needed beer. So, during World War II, an Icelandic brewery called Ölgerðin received special permission to make beer for the British Navy and later for the American troops stationed there, though it could not be sold to Icelanders. Bootleggers and black marketers thrived.

In 1983 the first "*beer bar*" opened up in Reykjavik. It sold a beer look-alike which was a mix of non-alcoholic beer and a shot of vodka. This ghastly combo became so popular that it too was made illegal.

Finally, on the 1st of March 1989, the ban on beer was lifted in Iceland. On that day, newly christened *The Beer Day,* over

320,000 cans were sold. Please note that there were only 260,000 Icelanders in existence at the time.

People guzzled beer without any particular increase in murder, pillage, or breakdown of the social order. Even so, at the time there were still a lot of people predicting the end of civilization in the wake of lifting the ban. Having seen how Iceland has evolved since then, they may not have been far off, some say.

Silly, stupid tourists.

"Let's have picnic on an iceberg," said a young tourist to his fellow travelers. And they did. They set up a card table and chairs, grabbed a couple of Polar Beers from their cooler, and climbed onto a berg that appeared to be solidly anchored to the shore. Now that's my kind of adventure! I came to Iceland expecting to see and feel the ice. Yes, I would be dumb enough to chock up that kind of intimate icy experience.

It all went well for the revelers until they found themselves marooned in the middle of the lake. The berg had floated away. Icebergs are totally unpredictable. They can flip without notice, they can break up or split. The kids could have slipped off the ice, and that would have been the end of them.

Almost 25 million acres of Iceland (about 11% of its surface area) is covered in glaciers. Some of these of these are melting and collapsing, creating deep lagoons where icebergs as large as a small county float. No tour of Iceland is complete without a boat ride at *Jökulsárlón*, a glacial lagoon seven miles square and still growing. No tour of the lagoon is complete without guides recounting the silly tourists story.

"People who do stupid things like that should be allowed to remove themselves from the gene pool. After all, this is Darwin at work," I heard someone say – and it could have been me.

Fortunately for the picnickers on ice, someone missed them and alerted the rescue folks. They became headline news, allowing Icelanders to say "Tourists!" in the way that implies they are a race of people with very low IQs.

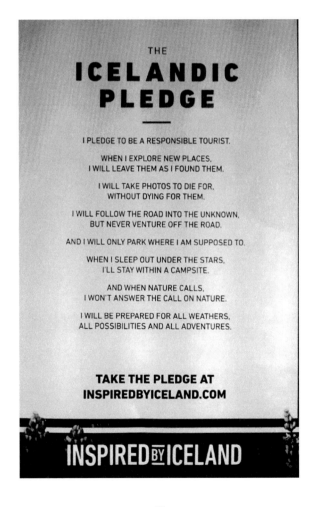

Jökulsárlón

Silly tourists aside, floating in our duck boat through these nature-carved ice sculptures was truly magnificent. The serenity, the strength and the elegance of ice as it does a slow dance in the lagoon transported me to a heavenly place. I didn't want to leave. If that was not enough, out of nowhere we came upon a seal pup taking a nap on its own personal ice floe. My cup overflowed with joy.

The bergs meander and melt, shape-shift, roll over and get buffeted by the wind. Slowly they pass through the narrow strait and out to sea. Some of them get washed back by the tides onto a nearby black sand beach, aptly named Diamond Beach. On the jagged icy surfaces, a million billion diamonds sparkled. One of bergs had inviting soft curves, and I couldn't resist spreading myself on it as though it were a lounge chair. That was second best to picnicking on a berg. Oh my, it's *wet!* Gosh it is hard. Not only that, it punished my bones as I tried to get up without sliding off into the icy surf that lapped at my heels. What did I expect of the 1000 year old super-compressed piece of ice? After all I am just a silly tourist with a low IQ.

Diamond Beach at Jökulsárlón

I live and you will live

It was Day Twelve already. We steamed towards the southern part of Iceland for one last stop at one of the earth's newer volcanic creations - the Westman Islands. The island of Surtsey only emerged from the ocean in 1963. It is a newborn compared to Heimaey, the only inhabited island, which poked its head out of its watery womb between five and ten thousand years ago, and it is still forming. As recently as 1973, a fissure ripped the island open. Fountains of fiery lava lit the skies for almost five months, as more of the island pushed itself up from the deep, leaving in its wake Mt. Eldfell. Some 400 homes and buildings got swallowed up by the ash.

The gods were smiling on the island community, because on the night of the eruption the entire fishing fleet happened to be in port due to bad weather. All the residents were evacuated, and for a while it looked as though the island had to be permanently abandoned. People did eventually move back, and today it is one of the most important fishing centers in all of Iceland, at least until the next eruption.

The setting of the town is spectacular, with rugged red brown bluffs on one side and two volcanic peaks on the other. Like everywhere in Iceland, Alaskan lupines were brought in and planted as a soil fixer and erosion control plant. The lavender purple flowers splash up and down the mountains and through town. As we wandered down the steps and pathways that have been built right along the edges of the new lava fields, we saw some of the skeletons of houses that had been dug out. It was hauntingly eerie, Pompeii like. All the pots and pans, shredded curtains and light fixtures were still in place, blackened by ash.

As I climbed Mt. Eldfell, I couldn't help but contemplate the absolute power of Nature, its violence, its serenity and its raw beauty. Right there at that moment I understood that it was Nature that regulates us and not the other way around, despite what Genesis says about us humans made in the image of God to have dominion over fish, birds, animals and the earth.

On our way back to the boat, we slowly made our way down to the cemetery, which had also been buried under many feet of ash but had been lovingly dug out by hand by a group of Norwegian students. Emblazoned in my mind was the picture of the archway as you entered the cemetery, charred and partially fallen, like an amputee. You could still read the inscription: *I live, and you will live.*

Heimaey: A third of the town was buried.

Westman Islands

Search and Rescue Heroes - the Landsbjörgers

"Mamma, I want to be a Landsbjörger when I grow up," say masses of Icelandic children as they watch their heroes on search and rescue missions, on live TV.

Action-filled high adventures, with the search and rescue folks scaling scary cliffs or risking their lives fording furious rivers;

supercharged trucks and sno-cats with floodlights and monster tires -- these light up the kids' dreams. The trucks are loaded with provisions and rescue equipment of course, from snow shovels and ropes to harnesses, search dogs and body bags. The Landsbjörgers are everyday citizens with the compassion and conviction of Mother Theresa, and the courage and strength of Spiderman. They rescue people who have fallen into deep crevasses; they dig out the family who has been trapped by an avalanche, and bring home the hiker stranded on a glacier trek when suddenly the wind came up and made frozen mashed potatoes out of him.

This is ICE-SAR, the *Icelandic Association for Search and Rescue.* They are the civilian saviors of Iceland, popularly known as Landsbjörgers.

They don't get paid to risk their lives. They lend their time, resources and expertise to save the lives of those in trouble and to help prevent accidents. They boast close to ten thousand members, with four thousand of them on active "callout" duty, on ninety-seven teams. They are totally self-funded and self-organizing, and are well trained and equipped. Most volunteers have daytime jobs, but their employers give them paid time off when called on a mission, just like jury duty. Many companies give them more than time off, like provisions and sometimes extra money to fund the rescue. Reverence for this group is up there with the gods and goddesses. The stories about their rescues are read avidly by all.

Looking for trouble and bringing it to a happily-ever-after ending is what Landsbjörgers do. It was they who rescued the silly tourists who picnicked on the iceberg. But they are feeling the pinch financially these days, as millions of naive tourists flood in, lured by the promise of easy access to adventure. "These hippies, they can be so stupid," one of guides told me. "They don't even bring a good arctic sleeping bag and they want to sleep under the stars. Then it freezes, the fog moves in, and we are called out to rescue them." The most common call for help is tourists driving rental cars and getting stuck and stranded in godforsaken places. *What were they thinking?*" It is a question often asked.

Many calls made to ICE-SAR are false alarms. A missing person shows up, surprised at all the fuss, or rescues himself before the rescuers arrive. Just the same, volunteers wait for the call to action, and show up even when there's none to be had:

How many Landsbjörgers does it take to screw in a light bulb?

Eight. One to screw in the light bulb, and seven to stand around hoping he falls, so they have something to do.

I too want to be a Landsbjörger when I grow up.

Homeward Bound

What I loved about the expedition is that we had to unpack just once, and we were a small group of twelve intrepid travelers. I loved the nightly lectures on the country's geology, its culture and history, and its flora and fauna. I'm so glad that most everything we did or ate was prepaid; I might have starved if I had to shell out $100 at every meal. But then again, now that I'm home I wouldn't be dealing with the consequences of the sumptuous nightly banquets that have attached themselves to my hips and waist.

Prices are high because they have to import everything, every piece of lumber, every nail, every Ziploc bag. The minimum wage is around $16. By the time we packed our bags to leave, that $350 hand knit sweater was beginning to feel like a bargain. ... No, I didn't buy one.

When we returned to Keflavik Airport to catch our onward flight, it seemed that all two million tourists were trying to leave Reykjavik at the same time. I could only move as fast as the crowd that jammed the stairways, the escalators, the bathrooms, the check-in and security lines. The airport itself was several sizes too small for the sheer number of passengers. There was not an empty seat in the house. The departure lounge was a total confusion of gates, restaurants, and duty free shops whose shelves were brimming with fluffy stuffed puffins, alcohol, and chocolates. There was nothing intuitive about where to go next, other than to be propelled by the crowds and hope that their destination was yours.

Boarding our delayed flight was strictly survival of the fittest. After standing in line for over an hour, tempers ran hot, rumors flew, passengers were ready to erupt. No announcements, no apologies for the delays. When the departure gate doors finally opened, we all elbowed and raced each other as though someone else might take our seats before we could claim them. This experience was a lousy ending to our trip, but the journey back allowed me plenty of time for taking stock.

Reflections

You're in for all sorts of surprises when you know absolutely nothing about a country before you arrive. The acerbic wit and the warmth and hospitality of the people we met were heartwarmingly remarkable, as was the 'I have your back' ethos, which is very strong in Iceland. I had expected more of a Northern European reserve, and a population that was fiercely independent and self-sufficient. This was not so. Icelanders, strong and smart as they might be, truly value and practice interdependence.

They are quick to help each other, and strangers too. The ICE-SAR team was the first to respond in Haiti, of all places, after the earthquake in 2010.

Icelanders tease and treat each other the same way as siblings who have shared a room for far too long -- a combination of loyalty, love and intolerance. None of this *I'm afraid I'll hurt your feelings, so I won't tell you that your deodorant has failed you.* No fear of getting sued either.

As the country's culture changes from hardscrabble rural to the plushy convenience of urban life; as Icelanders deal with a cultural shift from homogenous blue-eyed and blonde-haired folks to having increasing numbers of dark-haired, dark-eyed immigrants woven into their communities; as Icelanders reap the profits of the tourist industry, they are moving into a whole new chapter of their social history. This is a heady time of transitions, where possibilities abound. As they assimilate foreigners, will they become models for a multicultural society, or will fear and resentment tear their communities apart? Most certainly the influx of immigrants offers an opportunity to expand the gene pool.

Who knows when the next mountain will explode, or a flood from the melting ice cap will inundate villages and towns? Nature is very much in control on this island nation, and there is a humility borne of uncertainty. Today and this moment is all they have, and really all anyone has. Maybe the story of Grylla and her thirteen sons is a metaphor -- if we are not good enough to take care of our beautiful planet and of each other, we'll be carried off and boiled in Nature's cauldron.

I came as a tourist to this island that is marooned far out on the polar edge of the North Atlantic. I hiked and breathed in the raw landscape, from ice caps to volcanoes, from fields covered in Alaskan lupine to craggy coastlines. I left with a heightened sense of respect and love for our planet. There are no words that can describe those moments of deep appreciation and gratitude except to say that the earth goddess kissed me tenderly in my short sojourn in Iceland.

Bessastaðir Chapel. Revkiavik

Acknowledgments

As a traveler, I know only too well that if it were not for the generosity and kindness of the people I meet, I would have no story to tell. Thank you to all the Icelanders and guides who shared their stories and their beautiful country with David and me. Special thanks goes to Groa, who let me into her life and home with open arms and considered me a soul sister. I hope we will meet again.

Thank you to the staff of the Ocean Diamond, and to the fellow travelers of our Road Scholar group. Our paths crossed for just a twinkle, but the memories remain in my heart forever.

I am deeply grateful to my beloved writing group, the Frogs, who gave me endless encouragement and feedback on my manuscript. Thank you Ann, Ellen, and Jan for being my readers. I feel so privileged to be a part of this group.

Last but not least, I am eternally grateful to my comma and grammar police, my editor, my publisher and my husband of 42 years for never giving up on me, for always being there for me, and for giving birth to this book. I know I am your most difficult client . . . Thank you for putting up with me with love and laughter. This would not have come about without you.

With love and hugs to you all,

Asifa
October 2017

Also by Asifa Kanji

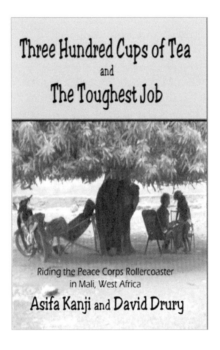

It's a crazy tale of vampire cats, giant termites and Toyota-flattening freight trains, not to mention playful conjugal text-message sex to pass those weary hours of waiting for the bush taxi. Most of all it is a story of the warm-hearted Malian people, set against a darker background of approaching famine and political unrest, and culminating in the couple's first-hand accounts of the military coup and Peace Corps evacuation from Mali in 2012. Told with humor and compassion, the side-by-side memoirs *300 Cups of Tea* and *The Toughest Job You'll Ever Love* take you on a 14 month journey of life in the Sahel.

About the Author

Asifa Kanji became locally famous by writing long travel letters that people actually liked to read. She's traveled in over 50 countries, letting serendipity take her by the hand. She has lived in a mud hut on the edge of the Sahara, in a dilapidated Italian villa in Asmara, in a loft apartment in Oslo. Her stories are quite fabulous. She is a writer, a hiker, a teacher, a henna artist, a returned Peace Corps volunteer, and a very good cook. Born in Dar-es-salaam, she grew up in Tanzania and Kenya, was schooled in England and followed her heart to America in 1975. She lives with her husband and travel companion David, in Ashland, Oregon.

68636610R00044

Made in the USA
Lexington, KY
16 October 2017